Bright Promises Dismal Performance:

AN ECONOMIST'S PROTEST

MILTON FRIEDMAN

Bright Promises Dismal Performance:

AN ECONOMIST'S PROTEST

Edited, with Introduction and Notes by
WILLIAM R. ALLEN

A Harvest/HBJ Book
Harcourt Brace Jovanovich, Publishers
San Diego   New York   London

Copyright © 1983, 1975, 1972 by Thomas Horton and Daughters

College Edition published by Thomas Horton and Daughters 26662 South New Town Drive, Sun Lakes, Arizona 85224

Trade Edition published by Harcourt Brace Jovanovich

Grateful acknowledgment is hereby given to *Playboy* magazine for the material on pp. 9–59; to *The Alternative: An American Spectator* for the material on pp. 60–75; to The Standard Oil Company for excerpts from *The Economics of Freedom* on pp. 141–152, and 161–168; to *U.S. News and World Report* for material on pp. 193–197; to *Wall Street Journal* for material on pp. 241–249; and to Newsweek, Inc. for all other articles appearing in this book. All material reprinted with permission.

Book designed by Mark Likgalter

Library of Congress Cataloging in Publication Data

Friedman, Milton, 1912–
  Bright promises, dismal performance.

  (A Harvest/HBJ book)
  1. Economics—Addresses, essays, lectures. I. Allen, William Richard, 1924–   II. Title.
HB171.F77 1983   330   82-21390
ISBN 0-15-114152-5
ISBN 0-15-614161-2 (pbk.)

Printed in the United States of America

  C D E F G H I J

CONTENTS

Contents

Implementing
Humphrey-Hawkins

March 5, 1979

The Humphrey-Hawkins "full employment" bill was passed in October 1978, by a vote of 70 to 19 in the Senate and by a standing vote, without a roll-call count, in the House. The overwhelming votes are decisive proof that the bill was all form and no content. It legislated ambitious goals—unemployment down to 4 percent by 1983, inflation down to 3 percent by 1983 and zero by 1988—but initiated no programs, leaving it up to the president and Congress to determine how to achieve the goals. Almost everyone could vote for the goals, and no one could object to the nonexistent means.

Recently, under the auspices of the National Tax Limitation Committee, a group of us drafted a proposed amendment to the Constitution of the United States designed to limit government spending. Though no one would associate the objective of limiting government spending with either Congressman Augustus F. Hawkins or the late Hubert Humphrey, I firmly believe that a by-product of adopting the proposed amendment would be to achieve the goals of the Humphrey-Hawkins bill.

Limiting Federal Spending . . .

Our draft amendment imposes a two-part limit on federal spending, one to apply if the Humphrey-Hawkins inflation goal of 3 percent is attained; the other if inflation is higher than that.

If inflation is 3 percent or less, the amendment permits federal spending to rise by the same percentage as dollar gross national product. If GNP grows from one year to the next by 5 percent (say 3 percent because of higher output and 2 percent because of higher prices), spending may also rise by 5 percent. If spending rose by the maximum permitted amount, it would remain a constant percentage of GNP—ending the persistent tendency for spending to absorb an ever-larger fraction of our income. In addition, if a thrifty Congress held spending below the maximum for any year, so that spending went down as a percentage of income, that lower level of spending would be the base for spending limits in future years. The result would be a permanent reduction in spending as a percentage of income.

If inflation is more than 3 percent, the amendment sets an even tighter limit. The permitted percentage in federal spending is reduced by one-quarter of the difference between inflation and 3 percent. For example, if GNP grows by 10 percent, of which 7 percent is accounted for by inflation, federal spending is permitted to rise by only 9 percent instead of 10 percent, forcing a decline in federal spending as a percentage of income so long as inflation stays at 7 percent.

The amendment does not require a balanced budget, but it certainly encourages one, in two different ways.

. . . Would Reduce Inflation . .

In the first place, deficits have occurred and grown primarily because there has been political pressure on Congress to increase spending but not taxes. A firm cap on federal spending would relieve that pressure. The deficit would disappear as economic growth raised tax receipts as a fraction of income, while the amendment kept spending constant or declining. Soon Congress would have the pleasant duty of reducing taxes in order to keep down the surplus.

Hypothetical calculations simulating the operation of the limit indicate that if the amendment had been in effect from 1969 to 1978, and if tax receipts and GNP had nonetheless been the same as they actually were, federal spending in 1978 would have been 17.7 percent of GNP instead of 22.6; and there would have been a cumulative surplus of $22 billion instead of a cumulative deficit of $271 billion.

This calculation gives a reasonable estimate of how the amendment would have affected spending as a fraction of income. However, it doubtless overstates the effect on the deficit. If the amendment had been in effect, inflation would have been lower. The same tax laws would have produced a lower effective tax rate, so tax receipts would have been less than they actually were. The deficits would clearly have been very much lower than they were, but not by as much as this calculation suggests.

In the second place, the amendment encourages a balanced budget by giving Congress and the administration a strong incentive to reduce inflation below the 3 percent level and to keep it there. Otherwise, they face the politically unpleasant task of forcing federal spending down as a percentage of income. The only way to reduce inflation is to reduce the creation of money by the Federal Reserve. The easiest way to do that is to reduce the size of the deficits that the Fed has been creating money to finance.

Together, these two effects could be counted on to achieve the Humphrey-Hawkins inflation goal in short order. We have had high inflation because it has been politically profitable for the powers that be to produce inflation. The amendment would make it politically profitable for the powers that be to reduce inflation. Inflation is made in Washington and can be eliminated only in Washington.

. . . and Unemployment

What of unemployment? Over the past decade, higher unemployment has accompanied higher inflation, and the relation has not been purely coincidental. Inflation has raised effective tax rates on income from all sources. Higher tax rates on wages have reduced the incentive for people to seek employment, reinforcing the effect of higher benefits to the unemployed in raising unemployment. Higher tax rates on business income have discouraged investment and reduced the incentive to offer employment. Erratic inflation has generated uncertainty about economic prospects that has further discouraged investment and impeded long-range business planning. These effects have been reinforced by the growing tide of regulation that has accompanied higher government spending. Under the circumstances, it is a tribute to the effectiveness of private industry that productivity has continued to increase, albeit at a snail's pace, rather than declining drastically.

Adoption of the amendment would end the growth in government spending as a fraction of income; it would end inflation; it would provide a more stable economic environment. Our creaking economy would be revitalized. Productivity and real income would resume their longtime rise; along with that, employment would increase and unemployment decline.

It would not be the first time that capitalist means were successful, and socialist means a failure, in achieving ends common to both those who favor capitalism and those who favor socialism.

Tax Cuts and Recession

May 12, 1975

Both opponents and proponents of the recent massive tax cut agreed that it would stimulate the economy. Opposition was solely to its size, based on the fear that large deficits would produce future inflation. Since its passage, the only doubts about its effectiveness that I have read were, "Would it work fast enough?"

The visible effect of the tax cut is that taxpayers have more funds to spend. They may not spend all, but they will certainly spend some, which raises demand for goods and services, and so is clearly expansionary.

But this is far from the whole effect. Taxpayers have more but the government has less. If government cuts its spending, that would offset extra spending by taxpayers. If government continues spending at the same rate—or, more realistically, increases spending at the same time that taxes are reduced—it must finance the part of its spending corresponding to the reduction in taxes by either borrowing from the public or creating new money through the Federal Reserve.

Suppose it borrows. Then the people who lend to the government have less to spend or to lend to others. In the first instance, this cancels the effect of the extra amount available to taxpayers. To take an extreme case which brings this out sharply: suppose taxpayers used all of their tax cut to buy government bonds. The direct effect of the tax cut would then be merely that taxpayers held government bonds instead of receipts for taxes paid! Indeed, even that indifference is partly illusory: by borrowing, the government has saddled each of us with an obligation to pay taxes in the future to pay the interest on the new borrowing (or to pay back the principal). The bonds that the taxpayers hold can be regarded as advance receipts for future taxes!

In practice, taxpayers will not lend all of the reduction in their taxes to the government. Government will have to borrow the rest at the expense of other borrowers: the government gets the funds instead of builders of houses, factories, and the like. Spending by taxpayers on consumption is higher, but spending on private capital formation is lower; more employment in the consumption sector, less in the investment sector.

Where is there any stimulus to the economy in this? Only at a more subtle level. Government can crowd out other borrowers only by forcing up the interest rate; the higher interest rate will make it more expensive to hold cash; additional spending by the public in an attempt to reduce cash balances will provide a net stimulus; but this is a once-for-all effect on total spending that empirical evidence suggests is minor.

If reduced tax receipts are replaced by the printing press or the accountant's pen—that is, by creating new money—the situation is different. Taxpayers benefiting from the tax cut spend more, and nobody else need spend less to enable government to continue spending. The catch is that this is like burning down the barn to roast the pig. The quantity of money can be increased without a tax reduction, and often has been, by Federal Reserve purchase of outstanding government securities. Such a monetary increase will have essentially the same effect—though perhaps with some minor differences in timing—as a monetary increase to replace tax receipts. Nonetheless, insofar as a tax cut does lead the Fed to increase the quantity of money more rapidly than it would otherwise have done, the cut is expansionary.

The emperor is naked. Yet I must confess that I favor tax cuts—not as a cure for recession but for a very different reason. Our basic long-term need is to stop the explosive growth in government spending. I am persuaded that the only effective way to do so is by cutting taxes—at any time for any excuse in any way. The reason is that government will spend whatever the tax system raises plus a good deal more—but not an indefinite amount more. The most effective way to force each of us to economize is to reduce our income. The restraint is less rigid on government, but it is there and seems to be the only one we have.

So hail the tax cut—but let's do it for the right reason.

Closet Keynesianism

July 27, 1981

In 1971 Richard Nixon signaled the end of an era, re-marking, "I am now a Keynesian." Recent headlines have trumpeted the "death" of Keynesianism and the rise of the "new" (i.e., old) theories of monetarism and supply-side economics.

However, deeply entrenched views die hard—as is demonstrated by a passage in a recent *Newsweek* (June 29) story on the economy: "Some economists question whether the United States really needs the stimulus that would be provided by Reagan's three-year tax-cut program. The danger is that by 1983 the nation could begin 'a renewed boom that can only push the basic inflation rate up to higher levels,' says economist George Perry of the Brookings Institution."

Are Tax Cuts a Stimulus? President Reagan's program calls for a reduction in government spending (really in the projected *increase* in spending) roughly equal in size to the reduction in taxes (really in the projected *increase* in taxes). According to simple-minded Keynesianism, a one-dollar cut in government spending reduces aggregate spending by one dollar, while a one-dollar cut in tax payments adds only a fraction of a dollar to spending, the balance being saved—which, as every good Keynesian knows, means hoarded under the mattress. Hence, the closet Keynesians should be attacking the president's program as *deflationary*, not as *inflationary*.

In terms of more sophisticated Keynesianism, or simply good economics, savings are not hoarded but are made available to borrowers—either the government or private borrowers, who in turn spend the amount borrowed. Hence, an equal cut in taxes and in spending is neutral in the short run—involving simply a shift from government spending to private spending. In the long run, it is a stimulus—but to output, not inflation. Since that part of private spending that is invested adds to productive capacity and hence to the future supply of goods, it will tend to reduce inflation. On this ground, too, the president's program is deflationary, not inflationary.

On simple Keynesian grounds, tax cuts that are larger than the accompanying cuts in government spending, and enough larger to offset the fraction of the tax reduction saved, are inflationary since private spending would go up by more than government spending would go down. Presumably, that prospect—no doubt expressed in the form of a 50- or 60-equation econometric model—underlies George Perry's comment.

On a more sophisticated analysis, even such tax cuts need not be inflationary. Everything depends on how the resulting government deficit (or increase in the deficit) is financed. If this is done by borrowing from the public, the excess of spending by government over tax receipts is balanced by a shortfall of spending by the private economy below its income receipts. And this result does not depend on how much of the tax reduction is saved. If the amount saved exceeded the deficit, pieces of paper evidencing the government's indebtedness would replace in the taxpayer's files pieces of paper certifying the payment of taxes. If the amount saved were less than that, the government would have to bid savings away from private borrowers. In the process it would raise interest rates, which would in turn reduce private investment. This "crowding out" would make the deficit essentially neutral with respect to aggregate spending, but would be inflationary in the long run because it would reduce private output.

The deficit is definitely inflationary only if it is financed by creating new money—in which case the excess of government spending over tax receipts is not balanced by a private shortfall. But the deficit need not be so financed. If it is, that is a failure of monetary policy, not of fiscal policy.

The Real Issue: One final—yet most important—comment. The analysis so far treats government spending and taxes as if they were two independent entities. They clearly are not. We know full well that Congress will spend every penny—and more—that is yielded by taxes. A cut in taxes will mean a cut in government spending. And there is no other way to get a cut in spending. That is the real reason why the big spenders and the big inflationists of the past have suddenly been converted to fiscal conservatism and to preaching the virtues of fighting inflation. They know that a multi-year tax cut will force multi-year spending reductions. They hope that a one-year tax cut will quiet public agitation and allow them to revert next year to their high-spending ways.

B. Taxation: Analytic Confusion, Political Hypocrisy and Reform

Whose Money Is It Anyway?

May 4, 1981

The controversy about President Reagan's proposed budget cuts tempts me to paraphrase the title of a Broadway hit and ask, "Whose money is it anyway?"

A revealing example is a statement attributed to the president of a local symphony in Muskegon, Michigan, complaining about proposed reductions in federal subsidies for the arts: "Psychologically, it would be wrong to go back to the people. They're being as supportive as they can." (*Newsweek*, March 16.)

Where does he think the federal subsidies come from, if not from the people? The federal government has no widow's cruse that provides subsidies at no one's expense. Strictly speaking, there are no federal funds, only taxpayer funds. Is it somehow "psychologically" right to extract funds from taxpayers by compulsion but wrong to appeal for voluntary support?

The Public Pays . . . The example is blatant because the subsidies in question—to the Corporation for Public Broadcasting and the National Endowments for the Arts and for the Humanities—are particularly indefensible. These activities have traditionally been supported by private funds in the United States. (I have received indignant letters from librarians who were apparently unaware that public libraries were established by Andrew Carnegie long before there was an income tax, let alone deductions for charitable expenditures.)

Moreover, they are primarily enjoyed by and benefit middle- and upper-income people. What justification is there for imposing taxes on low-income people to finance luxuries for high-income people? Only the political power of the elite who find it easier to persuade legislators to spend other people's money than to pay for their luxuries themselves. Of course, we shall be told that it is all for the "benefit" of the poor suckers who pay the taxes—their tastes must be uplifted, though how their tastes can be uplifted by TV programs they do not watch or books they do not read has always been beyond my understanding.

The case is fundamentally no different from the so-called "social programs" where cuts are said to harm the "poor." Most money spent on these programs does not go to the "poor," however defined. A large slice goes to well-paid government bureaucrats who administer the programs. Another slice goes to well-paid employees of the "nonprofit" agencies that have sprung up to guide and channel the use of funds, to do research on the programs and to lobby for their expansion. Still another slice goes to private interests that provide resources or garner contracts for projects such as public housing, urban renewal, and mass transit. What is left is divided between the "truly needy" and others who manage to qualify.* No one denies that the truly needy could be helped far more at far lower cost to the taxpayer if the categorical programs were abolished and replaced by a negative income tax that gave cash grants to persons with incomes below the level at which income taxes begin to be imposed. The reason that such a straightforward approach has not been adopted is because of the vested interests of many influential nonpoor in such "poverty" programs.

. . . and Pays: There remains the question, "Who pays?" It is an act of compassion for one human being voluntarily to give of his substance to another who is in need. But is it an act of compassion on A's part for him to force B to give assistance to C? For us as citizens to impose taxes on some poor people, as well as on ourselves, to benefit other poor people? The poor pay taxes too, and, if all taxes are taken into account, apparently as large a fraction of their income as those of us who are better off.

Yet in all the reams written about the harm that will be done by budget cuts, there is hardly a mention of who pays, or of the gain to the taxpayers from having to pay less. Is it really obvious that spending by government provides jobs and benefits while the same amount of spending by private individuals does not? To apply a remark of Adam Smith's about tariffs, the reverse of this "proposition is so very manifest, that it seems ridiculous to take any pains to prove it; nor could it

---

* A recent Census Bureau report estimates that 39.5 percent of households getting food stamps in 1979 were above the government's poverty line, as were 57.3 percent of those getting subsidized lunches, 53.4 percent of those in subsidized housing, 52.5 percent of those covered by Medicaid and 82 percent of those covered by Medicare.

ever have been called in question, had not the interested
sophistry of merchants and manufacturers and bureaucrats,
legislators and intellectuals confounded the common sense of
mankind."

High Living as a Tax Shelter

November 8, 1976

American tourists in London are often impressed by the number of Rolls-Royces cruising the streets and by the astronomical prices of second-hand Rolls-Royces: ten-year-old autos offered for sale at $30,000 or more. How can this display of luxury be reconciled, they ask, with Britain's economic difficulties? How can it survive Britain's highly egalitarian tax policies?

Rolls-Royce Roll

The answer is that those self-same tax policies, whatever their intentions, are a major cause of both the high living and the economic difficulties. Income from wealth—if received in cash form—is subject to tax at rates that reach 98 percent at the maximum. An Englishman of wealth has the alternative of buying a Rolls for, say, $50,000 in bonds or stocks or other financial forms. Suppose that he could invest in bonds yielding 15 percent—an extremely high rate even in inflation-plagued Britain. He would then get $7,500 in annual income. However, after paying tax at a 98 percent rate, he would have left only $150 to spend.

Suppose instead he buys the Rolls. The income he gets from it in the form of satisfaction and transportation is not subject to tax. His annual cost is the same as if he were renting the $50,000 car for $150 a year—surely, a tremendous bargain. Moreover, had he bought bonds, their value in terms of goods and services would depreciate each year as inflation proceeded and he would get nothing in return. The value of the car too may go down after allowing for inflation but at least he is getting the services of the car in return.

To cite one actual example. On a recent trip to Britain, we met a wealthy gentleman who owned a Rolls. He had purchased the car new twenty years ago for £8,000. He estimated its current sales price as £10,000. Of course, the £10,000 would buy much less in goods and services now than £8,000 would have bought twenty years ago. Yet there is hardly any financial investment that he could have made then that would not be worth fewer pounds today. And, in the meantime, he has been able to enjoy the services of a fine vehicle.

Not all Rollses cruising London streets are privately owned. Many are owned by business enterprises. But these too have been encouraged by taxes. An employee would rather receive the services of a car than an equivalent amount of cash, if the cash is subject to tax and the use of the car is not. Hence, this arrangement is often mutually advantageous to employer and employee.

What is true of Rollses is, of course, also true of luxury houses and apartments, paintings, jewelry—any form of wealth that yields services in kind rather than in cash. Moreover, the same forces also encourage lavish spending out of wealth on current services. Given confiscatory taxes on current income, and steeply graduated taxes on inheritances, the wealthy Briton might as well spend his capital on high living.

People and Capital Leave

But what has this to do with Britain's economic difficulties? A great deal. The wealthy man who wants to conserve his capital does so best by getting it out of the country. He has no incentive to use it productively within Britain. The ambitious man striving to become wealthy has no way of doing so unless he too can find tax shelters. There are many tax shelters in Britain as well as in the U.S. but, as here, the result is misdirection of such investment as does occur. An additional result is a brain drain of many of the ablest young men to countries where taxes are lighter.

The government has stepped in where private investment has no incentive to use it productively within Britain. The the capital flight produced by its own policies. It subsidizes private industry to replace the investment its own policies destroy.

The U.S. has not yet reached anything like the British situation. But we have been approaching it. Here, too, high living is perhaps the best, and certainly the surest, shelter available to the wealthy against both taxes and inflation. Here too, taxes reduce the incentive to invest, and distort the investment that does occur. These are "loopholes" it will stretch the ingenuity of the tax reformer to close—except by the most effective of all reforms, lower taxes.

When Is a Tax Cut Not a Tax Cut?

The answer to the question posed above is twofold:

1. When the so-called tax cut only offsets a rise in tax rates produced by the automatic effects of inflation; or

2. When the so-called tax cut is accompanied by a larger rise in government spending than in prices.

The second condition surely prevails today. The first very possibly may. So in spite of the flood of rhetoric about the need—or lack of need—for a tax cut, about what form the tax cut should take, and so on ad nauseam, the plain fact is that taxes are headed up, not down.

Suppose prices rise by 10 percent and your income also rises by 10 percent to match. It looks as if you are just keeping up with inflation. But you are not, because your personal income taxes will go up by more than 10 percent. The fixed dollar personal exemption of $750, as well as other fixed dollar items, will amount to a smaller fraction of your income, and your income will be pushed into higher dollar brackets taxed at higher rates.

Taxes and Inflation

In addition, if you have a savings account or if you own government or other bonds that pay interest, you will have to pay taxes on the whole of the interest even though the interest may not offset the fall in the real purchasing power of your principal; in effect, you are being taxed on a return *of* capital, not a return *on* capital. Similarly, if you sell stocks or real property, any gain in dollar value will be subject to tax even though the dollar gain may only offset inflation. If you have assets subject to depreciation, the tax law makes no allowance for the higher cost of replacing them.

All in all, if your income goes up by 10 percent, your taxes will, on the average, go up by about 15 percent. That is why, despite several supposed cuts in personal income taxes in the past decade, taxes paid were the same percentage of total personal income in 1976 as in 1966. The legislated tax cuts have been wholly offset by the unlegislated increases.

The effect of inflation on taxes makes inflation very attractive to the political authorities: they can propose and vote tax cuts while the effective tax rate goes up. How to have your cake and eat it too!

The way to end this fraud is to index the tax system, as has been proposed repeatedly. Congress has been quick to index its own salaries; it is time that it indexed our taxes.

Spending and Taxes

But there is a deeper layer of deception in the talk of a tax cut at a time when government spending is scheduled to increase more rapidly than prices. Suppose government spends $400 billion and raises $350 billion in funds labeled taxes. Who do you suppose pays for the $50 billion difference? The tooth fairy? Hardly. You do.

The real cost of government is measured by what government spends, not by the receipts labeled taxes. The goods and services it buys are not available for other use. If government finances its deficit by creating money, that imposes a hidden tax of inflation, in addition to raising explicit taxes. If it finances the deficit by borrowing, the government gets funds that would otherwise be available for building houses or factories or machines. In the process, it assumes a heavier burden of future interest payments, so that you can confidently look to higher taxes—open or hidden—in the future.

This same analysis demonstrates the fallacy in the talk about the "stimulative" effect of increased government spending. True, additional government spending adds directly to employment. But the reduction in funds for private use because of government borrowing to finance the spending—or the hidden tax of inflation imposed by money created to finance the spending—reduces the public's ability to provide employment. Governmentally financed employment simply replaces privately financed employment. The major effect is not to stimulate the economy but simply to expand the government sector at the expense of the private.

A far better way to stimulate the economy is to reduce government spending, taxes, and controls, leave more money in our pockets to spend or invest in accordance with our own values, and reduce distortions in the market that hinder us from doing so effectively.

Tax Camouflage

November 23, 1981

Philip Gramm is my guest columnist today, courtesy of a New York think tank that recently published Tom Hazlett's interview with Gramm ("Manhattan Report," International Center for Economic Policy Studies, October 1981). Phil Gramm—the Gramm of Gramm-Latta—is the Texas Democratic congressman who played a leading role in assuring passage of President Reagan's tax and spending cuts in the House of Representatives.

He was asked, "What's the deficit going to be like and what about people who claim that your tax cut is going to be inflationary?"

Philip Gramm: "The people who now claim that the president's tax cut will be inflationary and will contribute to the deficit are the same people who have continually voted in favor of deficit spending and increasing inflation during their congressional careers. So their concerns are quite hollow."

Late Converts: What Gramm says is true not only of some members of Congress but of the much broader group of Keynesians who have suddenly discovered the virtues of

313

balanced budgets. Though forecasting a recession, they are bemoaning deficits—when, on their principles, they should be calling for deeper tax cuts to stimulate the economy.

They oppose the tax cuts not because they are born-again budget balancers but because they remain what they have always been, namely, big spenders. They recognize that the widespread public opposition to budget deficits means that government spending is limited—even if not perfectly—by government revenues. The most effective way—indeed, I would say the only way—to keep down government spending is to keep down government revenues. Given the current public mood, the opponents of tax and spending cuts reluctantly concluded that they would have to accept them in 1981. However, they hoped that if the cuts could be limited to one year, or at most two, the fickle public would soon lose interest in tax cuts and they could resume their decades-old spending spree. They professed to be voting against "irresponsible" tax cuts. They really were voting for future spending increases.

That is also the force behind the renewed drive to rescind some of the tax cuts or to impose additional taxes now. Any real fiscal conservative who falls for that tactic will have demonstrated an utter inability to learn from experience.

Why so much pressure for increased spending, despite widespread agreement that simply throwing money at problems has seldom solved them and has generally made them worse?

Gramm: "I wrote an article a few months ago which, basically, was an explanation of the deficit. It went on to explain that the average spending bill we voted on in the last Congress cost about $50 million. The average beneficiary got between $500 and $700. There are 100 million taxpayers, so the average taxpayer paid 50 cents. You don't need a lot of economics to understand that somebody getting $700 is willing to do a lot more than somebody who is paying 50 cents. So, every time you vote on every issue, all the people who want the program are looking over your right shoulder and nobody's looking over your left shoulder. They're sending letters back home telling people whether Phil Gramm cares about the old, the poor, the sick, the bicycle riders . . . the list goes on. It's perfectly legitimate. The problem is that nobody's looking over the left shoulder.

"As an example, we had to vote individually on the twice-a-year cost-of-living adjustments for federal employees because a conservative Republican asked for a separate vote and, whereas it passed by 270-some-odd votes, only 59 people, approximately, voted for the cut on the floor. I received over a thousand letters in opposition to the cut. The largest National Association of Retired Federal Employees chapter in my district canceled the speech I was to give three days before the general election. They put my name in their national newsletter as one of their enemies . . . all of it perfectly legitimate. The problem is that we went out and did a survey in my district, and not one person in 10,000 who was not a federal employee knew how I had voted. So in being fiscally responsible under such circumstances, we're asking more of people than the Lord asks. At least I know if I do good—if I take the Bible literally—when I get to Heaven, it's going to be written in the Golden Book. I know here it will never be known."

Our New Hidden Taxes

April 14, 1980

The widespread tax revolt has already led seven states to adopt constitutional amendments limiting taxes or spending by state and local governments. Similar provisions are pending in most of the other states. It has led some thirty states to request Congress to convene a constitutional convention to propose an amendment requiring a balanced budget. It has led the National Tax Limitation Committee (NTLC) to draft an amendment to the U.S. Constitution to limit spending. The amendment has been introduced in Congress by bipartisan sponsors and has been endorsed by more than 1.2 million citizens who have signed petitions being circulated by the NTLC.

Washington Smoke Screen: Washington has reacted by mounting a rearguard offensive to obfuscate the issue. Meaningless congressional resolutions to cut spending have been accompanied by continued increases in taxes and spending. In addition, a major move is under way to increase concealed taxes in order to permit a much-trumpeted reduction of visible taxes.

Inflation is one form that move has taken. Inflation is not only a hidden tax, it is also a way to increase visible taxes without legislation through "bracket creep"—that is, by pushing taxpayers into higher income-tax brackets subject to higher rates. This tactic worked splendidly for a while. More recently, it has been generating opposition as the shell game has become crystal clear.

Accordingly, tactics have been shifting. One example is the endorsement of a value-added tax (VAT) by Senator Russell B. Long and Representative Al Ullman—the chairmen of the tax-writing committees of Congress. Because it would be collected by business enterprises, VAT would be concealed in the total price the consumer paid and hence not perceived as a direct tax burden. That is its advantage to the legislators—and its major defect to the taxpayers.

A more harmful example is the recently enacted excise tax on petroleum products, falsely labeled a "windfall profits" tax, which will further discourage domestic production of oil and increases our dependence on foreign oil. There is nothing whatever to be said for this disastrous measure—except that it provides tax funds for Congress to dispose of in a form that may avoid exacerbating the tax revolt.

More subtle examples are the "credit controls" imposed by the Federal Reserve at President Carter's request and the reserve requirements imposed by Congress on banks that are not members of the Federal Reserve System at the request of the Federal Reserve.

Credit Controls: No one refers to these measures as taxes, yet that is what they are. The "credit controls" require various financial intermediaries to hold non-interest-bearing reserves equal to 15 percent of the increase in their assets from a base date. That is precisely equivalent to levying a 15 percent tax on the income that, in the absence of the reserves, they would have earned from the increased assets. Though levied on the institutions, the tax will be shared between the depositors who supply funds to the institutions and the borrowers from the institutions. The tax discourages both saving and investment—what a way to foster growth!

This particular tax—because it is levied on the *increase* in assets—gives a windfall to the financial intermediaries themselves. This feature is confusing because of the complexities of the credit market, which defy the understanding of most citizens, so let me explain it by an analogy.

Suppose a tax were levied on retail sellers of shoes equal to 15 percent of the value of the *increase* in shoe sales over sales in 1979. No shoe store would have two prices—one for the "old" sales, one for "new" sales. All shoes would sell for the same higher price. Part of the extra receipts would go to the government; the rest to the shoe retailer. Is there any wonder that financial intermediaries are not complaining?

Similarly, the reserve requirement newly imposed on banks that are not members of the Federal Reserve System is *not* a credit-control measure. It is *not* required to enable the Federal Reserve to control the money supply. It is a straightforward tax on those banks—or rather, on their depositors, borrowers, and stockholders.

The taxload on the American people is too high. The tax revolt is fully justified. It will be a tragedy for the country if it is sidetracked by the replacement of open and visible taxes, and by delegating the power to impose taxes to government bureaucrats.

A Modest Proposal for 1984

December 10, 1979

Senator Eager-to-Be-Reelected introduced today a bill that would levy a Windfall-Profits Tax on Real Estate. The bill is cosponsored by twenty other senators.

Said Senator Eager in introducing the bill: "President Carter's imaginative initiative of five years ago attacking the windfall profits of big oil companies has been highly successful. It has generated revenue that has enabled us to finance ever bigger and better government programs to help the poor, the old, and the ill.

"Unfortunately, now that the last of the big oil companies has been nationalized, that source of revenue is disappearing. Much to everyone's surprise, the costs of the nationalized companies have risen much more rapidly than their revenues. They still enjoy a substantial excess of revenues over costs. However, that excess is barely enough to finance the growing budget of the Department of Energy—which has had to multiply its staff severalfold in order to administer the rationing of fuels and the control over their production that

Congress was farsighted enough to legislate along with the windfall-profits tax.

"Revenue is still available for social programs from the taxes being paid by the remaining small independent oil producers. Although that source has been growing, it is wholly inadequate to meet the pressing needs of our poor, our old, our ill."

Undeserved Gains: "We must find a new source of revenue. What better source than the obscene windfall profits that are being reaped by those privileged citizens who own their own homes? Their homes have risen in value by leaps and bounds—sometimes by as much as five or ten times the initial cost. As President Carter stated in 1977 with respect to oil companies, the homeowners 'have no equitable claim to that enhanced value because it is unrelated to their activities or economic contributions.' The enhanced value arises entirely from fortuitous changes in market conditions, from actions of Congress and the several states directed at preserving the environment, which have unfortunately limited new construction—from the bold anti-inflation action of Congress in holding down construction wages, which has unaccountably been followed by a shortage of construction labor—and from the continuing inflation that Congress has been powerless to curb despite our best efforts.

"We must end profiteering by one class of our citizens—however numerous—at the expense of the rest of us—however few. Greedy homeowners have been denying shelter to the needy. They have been shamelessly pushing prices to intolerable levels. Persons who have sold their homes at inflationary prices have not even reinvested the proceeds in building other homes and thus reducing the housing shortage. No, they have spent much of the proceeds on high living.

"These unearned gains by right belong to the people as a

whole, not to a selfish class of lucky homeowners. The bill I have introduced will make sure that the people as a whole get those gains."

A New IRS: "We cannot tap these unjustified windfall profits by waiting until the homes are sold and then taxing the profits realized. Selfish homeowners could readily evade such a tax by refusing to sell their homes. Fortunately, President Carter has shown us how to solve that problem: impose an excise tax on the product and label it a windfall-profits tax. That is what my bill does. It would impose a windfall-profits tax on owned homes equal to 50 percent of the annual rental value of the owned homes, as estimated by the Internal Rental Service of the U.S. Treasury Department. The tax would be payable quarterly along with the advance estimated payments on income tax. To avoid evasion by renting instead of owning, the same tax would be levied on all rents received from dwelling units.

"To protect the poor, the old, and the ill, my bill would exempt from this tax homes valued at less than $100,000, plus homes valued at less than $200,000, any of whose occupants are more than seventy-five years old or are permanently disabled or bedridden. In addition, it exempts homes owned by members of Congress, Cabinet officers, state governors and lieutenant governors, and senior civil servants.

"Enactment of this tax will end one form of shameless exploitation of the disadvantaged among us. It will enable us to finance on a sound, noninflationary basis, the social programs that the public demands. It will join President Carter's windfall-profits tax as a landmark in the progress of intelligent social reform."

The Kemp-Roth Free Lunch

August 7, 1978

Congressman Jack Kemp and Senator William Roth have introduced a bill to reduce sharply over the next three years tax rates on both individual and corporate income. They argue that lower rates will so sharply increase incentives to work, innovate, and invest that national output will rise apace and, as a result, so will the tax base and government revenue. In their view, lower tax rates can make possible higher government spending with lower deficits, can foster both higher consumption and higher investment—a free lunch for everyone.

I favor their bill—but I go only partway with their analysis of its likely effects.

Cost vs. Revenue

Some tax cuts can benefit both the Treasury and the taxpayer because of an important but neglected distinction between the *cost* of a tax to the taxpayer and the *revenue* it yields to the government. The capital-gains tax is a current widely discussed example. You may have an asset that you would like to sell but that you continue to hold because of the high capital-gains tax that selling it would generate under current law. You would be willing to pay something in order to sell it, but not as much as the current law demands. The government has, as it were, priced itself out of the market. A lower price, at which you found it desirable to sell, would leave you better off and produce revenue for the government. The revenue gain from such additional sales might more than compensate for the loss from sales made despite present taxes.

The top-bracket rates of the personal income tax are another example. Many taxpayers engage in activities that would otherwise be unprofitable in order to save tax. They buy tax shelters, say, that cost them, as they figure it, twenty-five or fifty cents on the dollar in order to save federal taxes of fifty to seventy cents and perhaps state taxes as well. At lower rates, they might well prefer to pay the tax and invest their funds in the most profitable ventures. They would be better off, and the government would get more revenue. Every time any one of us does one thing rather than another because the first produces a tax deduction while the second does not, we are illustrating the general principle.

Kemp-Roth might produce this kind of revenue gain. But an across-the-board cut such as they propose would, as they recognize, be unlikely to generate enough extra revenue from this source alone to compensate for the reduction in revenue from lower rates on currently taxed income. They count on a different free lunch—a larger tax base from the higher output stimulated by lower tax rates. Here, however, their argument falters.

The total tax burden on the American people is what the government spends, not those receipts called "taxes." Any deficit is borne by the public in the form of hidden taxes—either inflation or the even more effectively hidden tax corresponding to borrowing from the public.

If Kemp-Roth were enacted without a simultaneous reduction in government spending, the deficit would, at least initially, go up—and so would these hidden taxes. Lower explicit tax rates would foster efficiency and output; but higher hidden tax rates would encourage the waste of human energy and financial capital. We do not know the net effect, either on national output or on government tax receipts, corrected for inflation.

Limiting Spending

Why then do I favor Kemp-Roth? Because I believe that we are not getting our money's worth from the fraction of our income being spent for us by government, that the maintenance of both prosperity and freedom demand a reduction in the total tax burden. Moreover, I am persuaded by the experience of the past few decades that government will spend whatever the tax system will raise—plus a good deal more. The tolerable deficit has, unfortunately, been rising, but still it is not unlimited and does tend to inhibit spending. Hence, I have concluded that the only effective way to restrain government spending is by limiting government's explicit tax revenue—just as a limited income is the only effective restraint on any individual's or family's spending.

If the Kemp-Roth bill is a desirable measure, does it matter what the authors' arguments for it are? I believe that it does, that, despite the best of intentions, they harm the cause they seek to serve by offering bad arguments for a good measure.

Parkinson Revisited

July 12, 1976

Two decades ago, C. Northcote Parkinson formulated his famous first law: "Work expands so as to fill the time available for its completion." Later, he added the corollary: "Expenditure rises to meet income."

The just-published "Comparative Study of the Fiscal Systems of New Hampshire and Vermont, 1940–1974," by Professor Colin Campbell of Dartmouth College and his wife, Rosemary, provides a striking modern illustration. It would be hard to find a better pair of states for a comparative analysis.

Vermont and New Hampshire differ in one important fiscal respect. Vermont has both a state general income tax and a state general sales tax. New Hampshire has neither—indeed, it is the only state in the country with neither.

Expenditures vs. Services

The result: as Parkinson said, Vermont's expenditures have risen to meet its income. In 1974, state and local expenditures were 50 percent higher in Vermont than in New Hampshire as a percentage of the personal income of its residents. Vermont was the third most heavily taxed state in the Union; New Hampshire, the 47th.

Do Vermont citizens get proportionately more or better governmental services? The authors doubt it, on the basis of a careful examination of each category of expenditures.

In 1974, education absorbed 9.6 percent of personal income in Vermont vs. 6.6 percent in New Hampshire. Yet, teachers' salaries are higher in New Hampshire, years of school completed are roughly the same in the two states, and so are mean Scholastic Aptitude Test scores of high-school graduates. There is no sign of any significant difference in the quality of education, let alone a 50 percent higher quality in Vermont.

Welfare absorbed 3.1 percent of personal income in Vermont vs. 2 percent in New Hampshire, and according to the Campbells, "a principal reason . . . appears to be greater leniency in administration rather than higher welfare payments."

And so it goes, category after category: Vermont spends more; Vermont relies more on the state relative to the local community; and Vermont has little to show in return.

Taxes Are Habit-forming

Does Vermont's use of broad-based taxes reduce the burden of property taxes? Not at all. In 1974, property taxes averaged 6.6 percent of personal income in Vermont, 6.2 percent in New Hampshire—though in most earlier years there is a minor difference in the opposite direction.

Does the use of broad-based taxes mean that Vermont relies less on handouts from Washington? Quite the contrary. Vermont gets federal aid equal to 7.2 percent of its personal income; New Hampshire, 3.6 percent.

Does the use of broad-based taxes reduce the pressure on Vermont to borrow? Quite the contrary. The state and local debt is more than twice as large a percentage of personal income as in New Hampshire.

Apparently, extra income and sales taxes only whet the appetite of the ambitious public servant. In the private market, you generally get what you pay for—or you don't buy. The same force is present in local units of government. It is fairly easy to move out of a small community that is taxing much and returning little in services. However, the larger the governmental unit, the less the competitive pressure. That is why we get less for our tax money from the state than from the local government, and even less from the federal government.

The only way to cut government waste and extravagance is to cut government income.

After the Election

November 15, 1976

Public interest has naturally been focused on the presidential election. But I suspect that a little-noticed item on the Michigan State ballot may have greater significance for the long-run future of the U.S. than who is elected president.

That item, labeled Proposal C, provided for an amendment to the state constitution that would limit taxes imposed by the state government to a specified fraction (8.3 percent) of the personal income of the residents of Michigan in the prior fiscal year. Its other provisions were designed to assure that the limit is not rendered ineffective by the shift of functions from the state government to local communities without providing the necessary finances, or by the reduction of state grants to local communities. But the heart of the amendment is to enable voters to decide how much of their income they are willing to have the state of Michigan spend for them.

The Parts . . .

Do not the voters have that power without such an amendment? Yes and no. They elect representatives to legislatures and their representatives vote expenditures by strictly constitutional means. *But*—and it is a very big but—the political structure has a defect that biases results in the direction of larger total expenditures than the citizenry would vote for if it had the power to do so. The defect is that each spending proposal is voted on separately. The total budget is the sum of the separate appropriations.

In the case of each proposal separately, there tends to be a small group—which we call a special-interest group if we are not members of it—that has a large stake in its adoption. The cost is spread thinly over all taxpayers. Each special interest has every reason to spend heavily and to work hard for the adoption of its pet proposal. No taxpayer has a strong interest to oppose the measure. (A dramatic case on the federal level is the $600 million annual subsidy to the Merchant Marine, amounting to $12,000 per year for each of the 50,000 persons employed in the industry. No wonder the maritime unions are willing to make large political contributions and to lobby vigorously for such subsidies. On the other hand, the cost of each person in the U.S. comes to about $3 a year. What taxpayer will regard saving that sum as a sufficient reason to vote against his representative?)

This defect in our political structure is present at both state and federal levels. Programs have been adopted by an unholy coalition of well-meaning reformers and self-interest groups. Once adopted, they have invariably disappointed the well-meaning reformers. Instead, they have been captured by special interests that the reformers would never knowingly have supported.

The result has been a ballooning of government spending—from about 10 percent of the national income in 1928

329

(two-thirds state and local) to about 40 percent today (two-thirds federal). How many taxpayers—even those who benefit from one special-interest provision or another—believe they are getting their money's worth?

. . . and the Whole

Proposal C was designed to rectify this defect. It gave the taxpayer a chance to vote on the budget as a whole and to keep from being nickeled and dimed to poverty by the piling on of one piece of special-interest legislation after another.

The need for such an amendment could not be better demonstrated than by the frantic efforts of its opponents. The Michigan Education Association spearheaded the opposition and raised a substantial slush fund (rumored to be $300,000 to $500,000) to spread flat misstatements about the proposal—statements that if made by a commercial firm would surely justify prosecution under truth-in-advertising legislation. Why did they do so? Look at the record. Spending on schooling has been rising all over the country. At the same time, the performance of students has been declining. Both are the common result of a shift of control from local communities to the states and from the states to the federal government. The farther the source of funds from the local community, the easier it is for a concentrated interest to exert political pressure, and the harder it is for the taxpayer to exercise effective control over how his money is spent.

Another dramatic example of the attitude of the opponents is the following excerpt from an editorial in the *Detroit News* in opposition to the amendment:

". . . Taxpayers don't want to pay much.

"The more pertinent point is that government must spend what is necessary for the public welfare—not what we as individual taxpayers would like to contribute."

Who, if not the taxpayers, should decide "what is necessary for the public welfare"? The officials of the Michigan Education Association? The editor of the *Detroit News*?

This is a call for an authoritarian government, an explicit rejection of democratic self-government. The editorial writer has let his special interest in inducing taxpayers in the rest of Michigan to subsidize Detroit get the better of his political beliefs. When he comes to his senses, he will be as appalled as I am at what he has written.

The tax-limitation proposal first saw light in California in 1973, when it was put on the ballot as Proposition 1, by a statewide petition drive led by Governor Reagan. It was finally defeated, after a campaign of misrepresentation and confusion like that in Michigan, spearheaded there by the political opponents of Governor Reagan as well as the same kind of special-interest groups active in Michigan.

This year Michigan is the only state in which a tax-limitation amendment was on the ballot, though active movements are under way promoting similar amendments in a dozen or so states, as well as at the federal level.

Another Setback

I'm dismayed to have to report that Proposal C was defeated. In the State of Michigan, as in California three years ago, government employees and other special-interest groups have succeeded in bamboozling the naive taxpayer, in making him believe that down is actually up. This second defeat is no reason for giving up. On the contrary, the ability of those who feed at the public trough to persuade the taxpayer that Proposal C would raise his taxes rather than lower his taxes is the strongest possible indication of the need for a constitutional amendment that would curb their power.

We must redouble our efforts. Unless we can limit the cancerous growth in government, unless we can stop the shift of power from city hall to Statehouse, and from Statehouse to the White House, there is little hope of maintaining a free political system. The longer the delay, the harder the task, because the tribe of bureaucrats grows apace.

I am moved to paraphrase the call of the "Internationale": "Arise ye prisoners of taxation, you have nothing to lose but the IRS."

The Uses of Hypocrisy

September 13, 1982

The reaction to the Senate's passage of a constitutional amendment to balance the budget and limit taxes reminds me of William F. Buckley's brilliant remark that he would rather be governed by the first 1,000 names in the Boston telephone directory than by the faculty of Harvard.

Commentators vs. the People: Commentators from the right and the left have alleged that the Senate action is sheer hypocrisy. A president who submitted budgets implying massive deficits and a Senate that voted for them now support a constitutional amendment requiring a balanced budget! The Congress and the president have the power to enact a balanced budget. So why do we need an amendment?

At the same time, every poll shows that 75 percent or more of the public favor the balanced-budget tax-limitation amendment. Who is right?

The critics are right in what they allege. But the public is right about the importance of passing the amendment.

Of course, the president and the Congress have the power to enact a balanced budget. They also would have the power to maintain freedom of speech without the First Amendment. Yet I have read no columnist—however caustic his comments on Congress's hypocrisy—who has suggested that the First Amendment serves no purpose and should be repealed.

Of course, the Senate is guilty of hypocrisy in voting simultaneously for a large current deficit and for a constitutional amendment to prevent future deficits. The hypocrisy of Congress is the only reason that there is any chance to get Congress to pass an amendment limiting Congress. Most members of Congress will do almost anything to postpone problems. That is why Social Security is in such a financial mess. If the hypocrisy did not exist, if Congress behaved responsibly, then there would indeed be no need for an amendment. Congress's irresponsibility is at one and the same time the reason we need an amendment and the reason that there is a chance of getting one.

Hypocrisy may lead to the passing of the amendment. But that will not prevent the amendment, if passed, from having important effects three or four years down the line—and from casting its shadow on events even earlier. Congress will not lightly violate the Constitution. Members of Congress will wriggle and squirm. They will seek, and no doubt find, subterfuges and evasions. But their actions will be affected significantly by the existence of the amendment. The experience of several states that have passed similar tax-limitation amendments provides ample evidence to that effect.

Some critics have given the impression that the amendment was hastily knocked together to meet the need for a fig leaf. That is not the case. The amendment had its origins a decade ago—in a California proposition that failed but passed later in an improved form (not Proposition 13). A widely representative drafting committee of the Natonal Tax Limitation Committee produced a draft in January 1979. The National

Taxpayers Union contributed its version. The Senate Judiciary Committee produced the final version more than a year ago after lengthy hearings and with the active cooperation of all the major contributors to the earlier work. In my opinion, the final version is better than any earlier draft.

What the Amendment Does: It is important to be clear what the amendment does and does not do. Like the first ten amendments, it does limit the power of Congress in order to free the people—in this case, from excessive taxation.

It does *not* mandate a balanced budget. It provides rather that Congress may *plan* a deficit only if it explicitly votes to do so by a supernormal majority (three-fifths of the elected members of both houses).

It does *not* prevent taxes and spending from rising faster than national income. Rather, such an increase requires Congress to vote specific taxes that will yield the requisite amount by a constitutional majority (a majority of the elected members and not merely of those present and voting).

The amendment does not introduce any new economic theory into the Constitution. It does not even change the present budget process *if* Congress enacts a balanced budget that rises by no greater a percentage than national income. But it does stiffen the requirement for passing a budget that is in deficit or for raising the fraction of our income spent on our behalf by the government.

The amendment is excellent. We shall all be well served if it is passed promptly. At the same time, it will not bring nirvana.

How Flat Is Flat?

August 2, 1982

A recent surge of interest in replacing the present income
tax by a flat-rate tax has elicited two predictable reactions:
first, the surfacing of the old myth that, in the words of Tom
Wicker, "the result [of a flat-rate tax] would be a massive
redistribution of income, with more of the tax burden shifted
from the rich to the poor and middle class"; second, the use
of the rhetoric of flat rates as a disguise.

The Myth: A true flat-rate tax has two components: first, a
single tax rate applicable to everyone and to the whole of the
tax base; second, a tax base equal to total income with no
deductions except personal exemptions and strictly defined
expenses of earning the income. If present personal exemptions were retained, a rate of not more than 15 or 16 percent
would yield the same revenues as the present system with its
rates of 12 to 50 percent. If present personal exemptions were
raised substantially—as they should be in view of the extent
to which their real value has been eroded by inflation—a
somewhat higher rate, perhaps 17 percent, would be required
to raise the same revenue.

336

Contrary to Wicker, the poor, middle class, and rich would all gain from the substitution of a true flat-rate tax for the present income tax. The poor would pay less tax because of high personal exemptions. Many in the middle class would pay less tax because of a lower rate. Others in the middle class and the rich would pay more tax to the government yet be better off. They would pay more because the lower rate would render present costly tax shelters unattractive. They would be better off because their gain from being free to use their assets in the most productive instead of the most tax-evasive way would be larger than the extra tax. Tom Wicker's mistake is his failure to recognize how large a wedge there is between the taxes paid and what it costs taxpayers to pay and avoid or evade taxes.

Rhetoric: The flat-rate tax is clearly a splendid idea. However, it also arouses intense opposition from powerful special interests created by the existing tax system: recipients of so-called charitable contributions, homeowners, the housing industry, institutions financing housing construction, the myriad other producers of and beneficiaries from tax shelters, tax lawyers and accountants, and, last but not least, politicians who raise campaign funds from special-interest groups seeking to retain existing tax loopholes or to create new ones.

A formidable lobby, indeed, which is why I have for decades tempered my enthusiasm for a flat-rate tax with a realistic recognition that it does not have the chance of the proverbial snowball.

Bills labeled "flat rate" have been pouring into a legislative hopper. Some provide for a true flat rate. Most have only the label. They retain major deductions and keep graduated rates. For example, Senator Bill Bradley and Congressman Richard A. Gephardt have introduced a much-publicized bill for a "flat-rate tax" that would retain deductions for contributions, interest paid on owned homes, state and local taxes, and income from Social-Security and veterans' benefits. It also would have rates running from 14 percent to 28 percent—or a top rate double the bottom rate. A far cry from a true flat rate.

'Left' and 'Right': Nonetheless, such proposals seem extremely attractive. They offer a compromise between the so-called left and right. The left might accept a lower top rate as the price of gaining a broader base. The right might accept a broader base as the price for gaining a lower top rate.

However, appearances are deceiving. Such a compromise is neither desirable nor feasible. Neither side would trust the other and both are right. If it were ever enacted, the left would go to work to raise the rates—and they would quickly be joined by persons on the right pleading fiscal necessity. The right would go to work to broaden the deductions—and they would quickly be joined by persons on the left pleading equity and social priorities. After all, that is how we got into our present fix. History would simply repeat itself.

There is, I believe, only one way to make a bargain stick: by amending the Constitution to require that any income tax must be levied at a flat rate with no deductions from the tax base other than personal exemptions and expenses of earning the income.

We seem to be well on our way to enacting a constitutional amendment to balance the budget and to limit taxes. Perhaps the time has come to take the next step and outlaw the outrageous kind of income tax from which we now suffer.

C. Welfare

Leonard Woodcock's Free Lunch

April 21, 1975

In a statement on national health insurance, Leonard Woodcock, president of the United Auto Workers, is reported to have said that "if the bill is enacted no American ever again would have to pay a doctor's bill or a hospital bill."

Who does Mr. Woodcock think would pay the bill? The Arab sheiks? He surely knows better. He knows that laundering the money we pay through Washington is simply a different—and more expensive—way to pay our hospital or doctors' bills than paying them directly.

A minor puzzle is how an intelligent man like Mr. Woodcock can talk such nonsense. It is truly a remarkable tribute to our ability to become prisoners of our own rhetoric.

The major puzzle is how an intelligent man like Mr. Woodcock can support a measure that is against the interest of U.S. citizens in general, of members of his own union, and even of the officials of that union.

Why All Would Lose

Consider union members first. The UAW is a strong union and its members are among the highest-paid industrial workers. If they wish to receive part of their pay in the form of medical care, they can afford, and hence can get, a larger amount than the average citizen. But in a governmental program, they are simply average citizens. In addition, a union or company plan would be far more responsive to their demands and needs than a universal national plan, so that they would get more per dollar spent.

As to union officials, if they established a union plan, or negotiated a company plan, they would get the credit. They might also get credit for the enactment of a national plan, but, once enacted, they would have nothing special to do with it, and they would have to look for other ways to justify their well-paid existence.

For the nation, national health insurance would be an expensive disaster that would reduce the quality of medical care and would hurt especially the poor. This proposition is supported by our own experience and by the experience of other countries.

In 1960, before Medicare and Medicaid, total spending in the U.S. on health care amounted to 5 percent of the gross national product. Today, it amounts to 8 percent. Spending by government accounted for 25 percent of the 5 percent, but for 40 percent of the 8 percent, so we are already nearly halfway to totally socialized medicine. To judge from the continuing complaints, the quality of medical care has shown no comparable rise. Higher government spending has mostly gone to raise the incomes of physicians and other health-care personnel, pay for the duplication of expensive equipment, and support other forms of waste. Indeed, much pressure for national health insurance reflects the perceived failure of Medicare and Medicaid, and the mistaken belief that this failure can be remedied by buying these programs in a still larger program.

When medicine appears to the user to be a "free" good, there is no limit to the amount demanded. Yet there is a limit to the amount available. Inevitably, people who are well connected, hypochondriacs with time on their hands, and the simply persistent get an undue share. Inevitably, a physician, however conscientious, who is harried by patients with no incentive to restrain their demands, is forced to dilute the quality of medical care. Inevitably, governmental guidelines replace his judgment in deciding who gets medical care and who goes to the end of the queue.

A Cautionary Tale

Britain's experience with its National Health Service is a premonition of what would happen here. British physicians have clearly been unhappy with the system: since 1966, the number emigrating each year has equaled a third of the annual output of Britain's medical schools. But patients too have been unhappy: 2 million British citizens are not only paying compulsory medical levies but also subscribe to private medical insurance, and the number is growing rapidly. Government hospitals are old, overcrowded, and understaffed—more than two-thirds of the hospitals now in use were built in the nineteenth century! The delay for a tonsillectomy averages twenty-two weeks and much longer delays are common for serious but postponable operations. As a result, private hospitals or their equivalent have been burgeoning.

This is the kind of system that well-meaning people like Mr. Woodcock are leading us to. Is there no way we can induce them to check their rhetoric against reality?

Where Has the 'Hot' Summer Gone?

August 4, 1975

Reported unemployment has now been around 9 percent for four months. In advance, such a development would have been regarded as certain to produce a "hot" summer replete with urban riots and Washington hysteria, and also to overwhelm any concern about inflation in the mad rush to do everything and anything to reduce unemployment. Yet it has produced little more than a ripple on the social or political scene. The cities are quiet—if broke. There is no public outcry. President Ford rises in popular esteem by vetoing spending measures advertised as directed at reducing unemployment and his vetoes are upheld. Inflation remains *a* if not *the* major concern of the public.

How come? What went wrong with the conventional wisdom?

The answer, I believe, is that the recorded level of unemployment is highly misleading. It does not mean what it is taken to mean, and it does not mean the same thing today as it did in the past.

Employment vs. Unemployment

Instead of looking at how empty the glass is, let us look at how full it is. At the peak of the boom, in October 1973, 58.9 percent of all persons in the United States 16 years of age and over and not in institutions had jobs (including self-employment). This percentage hit its lowest point for the current recession some months ago, in March, when 56.4 percent had jobs—a decline of only 2.5 percentage points. At its low point, the percentage was higher than the low reached during three of the five earlier postwar recessions (the exceptions are 1954 and 1970). By this standard, the current recession is the third mildest of the six postwar recessions. No reason there for a hot summer.

The reported unemployment figures tell a very different story. They doubled from 4.5 percent in October 1973 to 9.2 percent in May of this year, far above the prior postwar peak of 7.5 percent reached in October 1949. By this standard, the current recession is by far the most serious of the six postwar recessions. Every reason for a hot summer.

What explains the difference between the employment and unemployment figures? For one thing, there has been a sizable expansion in employment opportunities in recent years. More teenagers, more women, have sought and found employment. The number of persons seeking jobs has risen along with the number of jobs available. What is called the "labor force" has grown even more rapidly than the number of persons employed. As the recession deepened, and jobs became less plentiful, some job seekers became discouraged and left the labor force, but an even larger number of persons began to look for jobs to replace or supplement the earnings of other family members. One-third of the persons currently counted as unemployed have either newly entered or reentered the labor market. Paradoxically, the high reported level of unemployment is in part a sign that jobs are available and that it is worthwhile to look for them.

Statistics of Unemployment

In addition, the high reported levels of unemployment are partly a statistical artifact reflecting expanding government programs to assist the unemployed.

Consider someone who leaves a job intending to remain out of the labor force for a time—a woman planning to have a child, a youngster returning to school, an oldster retiring, or even someone wanting to take a few months' vacation. If the formalities can be satisfied, all can be eligible for unemployment insurance—and one of the formalities is that the person be available for employment. At a time like this, no one is likely to question eligibility on these grounds. (For example, through an interstate agreement many residents of New York, Michigan, and other states pick up their unemployment checks in Florida.) Schoolteachers on nine-month contracts may qualify in many states for unemployment insurance in the summer months. No doubt, if asked about their status, they would report themselves as seeking work, and so be counted as unemployed.

Anecdotes are not proof, but they illustrate the principle that changes in social arrangements that have made unemployment more attractive have also tended to increase the number of persons who so record themselves.

No one who lived through the Great Depression can doubt the searing personal costs of unemployment, the tragedy that strikes when an able-bodied head of a family cannot find a job that will enable him to discharge his responsibilities and maintain his self-respect. The recession has certainly increased the number of persons who suffer this tragedy and there is no gainsaying the great harm it has done.

Human Cost of Unemployment

At the same time, all unemployment is not of this kind. The growth of government transfer payments in the form of unemployment insurance, food stamps, welfare, social security, and so on, has reduced drastically the suffering associated with involuntary unemployment. A worker who has been laid off and expects to be recalled after a reasonable interval, as most laid-off workers are, may enjoy nearly as high an income when unemployed as when employed. He need pay neither social security nor personal income taxes on his unemployment benefits, and he is spared commuting and other job-related costs. At the very least, he need not be so desperate to find another job as his counterpart was in the 1930s. He can afford to be choosy and to wait until he is either recalled or a more attractive job turns up. The result is to swell the number reported as unemployed without any corresponding increase in personal distress.

The report that 8 million persons are unemployed conjures up the image of 8 million persons fruitlessly tramping the streets looking for a job. That is a false picture. Most people recorded as unemployed are between jobs or between entering the labor force and finding a job. Most are in families that have one or more other earners. Most receive some income while unemployed. Each week more than half a million find jobs, while some half-million other people begin to look for jobs. A major effect of the recession has been to lengthen the time it takes to find a job—from an average of about ten weeks in 1973 to about fifteen weeks today.

Unemployment is certainly a serious problem, but we must not be misled by ambiguous statistics. The public's calm about unemployment is not a deceptive puzzle. It is a revealing and accurate measure of the true dimensions of the problem.

Negative Income Tax—I

September 16, 1968

The negative income tax, as Paul Samuelson remarked in one of his recent columns (*Newsweek*, June 10), is a striking example of an idea whose time has come. First suggested decades ago, it has attracted widespread interest only in the past few years as the defects of present methods of assisting the poor have become more obvious and more flagrant.

The widespread interest is remarkable. But the appearance of growing agreement—of support for a negative income tax by the right and the left, by businessmen and professors, by Republicans and Democrats—is highly misleading. In large part, it reflects the use of the same term to describe very different plans. For example, some months ago, more than 1,200 economists from 150 different colleges and universities signed a petition favoring a negative income tax. Despite my longtime advocacy of a negative income tax, I found it impossible to join in sponsoring the petition or even to sign it because I did not agree with the plan it advocated or the arguments it presented.

A Specific Plan

The basic idea of a negative income tax is to use the mechanism by which we now collect tax revenue from people with incomes above some minimum level to provide financial assistance to people with incomes below that level.

Under present law, a family of four (husband, wife, and two dependents) is entitled to personal exemptions and minimum deductions totaling $3,000 ($2,400 personal exemptions, $600 deductions).

If such a family has an income of $3,000, its exemptions and deductions just offset its income. It has a *zero taxable* income and pays no tax.

If it has an income of $4,000, it has a *positive taxable* income of $1,000. Under current law, it is required to *pay* a tax of 15.4 percent, or $154. Hence it ends up with an income after tax of $3,846.

If it has an income of $2,000, it has a *negative taxable income* of −$1,000 ($2,000 minus exemptions and deductions of $3,000 equals −$1,000). This negative taxable income is currently disregarded. Under a negative income tax, the family would be entitled to *receive a fraction* of this sum. If the negative tax rate were 50 percent, it would be entitled to receive $500, leaving it with an income after tax of $2,500.

If such a family had no private income, it would have a negative taxable income of −$3,000, which would entitle it to receive $1,500. This is the minimum income guaranteed by this plan for a family of four.

Let me stress the difference between the *break-even income* of $3,000 at which the family neither pays taxes nor receives a subsidy and the *minimum guaranteed income* of $1,500. It is essential to retain a difference between these two in order to preserve an incentive for low-income families to earn additional income.

Let me stress also that these numbers are all for a family

of four. Both the break-even income and the minimum guaranteed income would be higher for larger families and lower for smaller families. In this way, a negative income tax automatically allows for differences in need because of differences in family size—just as it does for differences in need because of differences in income.

This plan is intended to replace completely our present programs of direct relief—aid to dependent children, public assistance, and so on. For the first year or two, it might cost slightly more than these programs—because it is so much more comprehensive in coverage. But, as the incentive effects of the plan started to work, it would begin to cost far less than the present exploding direct-assistance programs that are creating a permanent class of people on welfare.

Alternative Plans

By varying the break-even income and the negative tax rate, by adding the negative income tax to present programs rather than substituting it for them, it is possible to go all the way from the rather modest and, I believe, eminently desirable plan just outlined to irresponsible and undesirable plans that would involve enormous redistribution of income and a drastic reduction in the incentive for people to work. That is why it is possible for persons with so wide a range of political views to support one form or another of a negative income tax.

Negative Income Tax— II

October 7, 1968

The proposal to supplement the incomes of the poor by paying them a *fraction* of their unused income-tax exemptions and deductions, which I termed a *negative income tax* years ago, has many advantages over present welfare programs:

1. It would help the poor in the most direct way possible.

2. It would treat them as responsible individuals, not as incompetent wards of the state.

3. It would give them an incentive to help themselves.

4. It would cost less than present programs yet help the poor more.

5. It would eliminate almost entirely the cumbrous welfare bureaucracy running the present programs.

6. It could not be used as a political slush fund, as so many current programs—notably in the War on Poverty—can be and have been used.

In the course of advocating a negative income tax like the one I outlined previously (*Newsweek*, September 16), I have repeatedly encountered the same objections time and again. Let me try to answer a few of them.

1. *By removing a means test, the negative income tax establishes a new principle in the relation between citizens and the government.* This is simply a misunderstanding. The negative income tax retains a means test—the straightforward numerical test of income rather than the present complex and demeaning test. It uses the same means test to decide who shall receive assistance from the government as the one we now use to decide who shall pay the expenses of government.

True, it guarantees a minimum income to all. But that is not a new principle. Present welfare arrangements guarantee a minimum income in practice, and in some states, even in law. The trouble is that these present welfare programs are a mess.

2. *The minimum levels of income proposed are too low.* We are talking about a federal program and a *nationwide* minimum. The levels of assistance are decidedly higher than current levels in most states. They are decidedly lower than current levels in states like New York, Illinois, and California. It would be absurd to enact such high levels as national standards. But there is every reason to encourage the more affluent states to supplement the federal negative income tax out of state funds—preferably by enacting a supplementary state negative income tax.

3. *The poor need regular assistance. They cannot wait until the end of the year.* Of course. The negative income tax, like the positive income tax, would be put on an advance basis. Employed persons entitled to negative income tax would have supplements added to their paychecks, just as most of us now have positive taxes withheld. Persons without wages would file advance estimates and receive estimated amounts

due to them weekly or monthly. Once a year, all would file a return that would adjust for under- or over-payments.

4. *The negative income tax destroys incentives to work.* Under present programs, persons on welfare who obey the law generally lose a dollar in relief for every additional dollar earned. Hence, they have no incentive whatsoever to earn the dollar. Under the negative income tax plan that I propose, such a person would keep fifty cents out of every additional dollar earned. That would give him a far greater incentive than he now has.

One additional point. A welfare recipient now hesitates to take a job even if it pays more than he gets on welfare because, if he loses the job, if may take him (or her) many months to get back on relief. There is no such disincentive under a negative income tax.

5. *The negative income tax will foster political irresponsibility.* If we adopt an open and aboveboard program for supplementing the incomes of people below some specified level, will there not be continued political pressure for higher and higher breakeven incomes, for higher and higher rates on negative income? Will the demagogues not have a field day appealing to have-nots to legislate taxes on haves for transfer to them?

These dangers clearly exist. But they must be evaluated in terms of the world as it is, not in terms of a dream world in which there are no governmental welfare measures. These dangers are all present now—and have clearly been effective. The crucial question is, how do we get out of the mess into which these pressures have driven us? The negative income tax offers a gradual and responsible way to work ourselves out of this mess. No other way of doing so has as yet been suggested.

VI. International Economics

A. Trade, Protectionism, and Embargoes
B. The Balance of Payments and the
   Value of Currencies
C. Two International Case Studies

INTRODUCTION

Although the huge American economy has long been significant in the commerce of the rest of the world, foreign trade has not bulked large in United States aggregate economic activity. It is now bulking larger. International trade has been expanding more rapidly than domestic economies, increasing more than sixfold from 1970 to 1980. And, over the same period, United States imports have more than doubled as a proportion of gross national product, now over 12 percent.

The essential logic of production specialization and exchange is the same for people who live in different countries as it is for those in the same country. Internationally as well as domestically, we live best by producing on the basis of relative efficiencies and trading in unrestricted markets, with the gain from trade stemming directly from imports, not exports.

To channel and constrain production and exchange by government taxes, restrictions, and directives is to stymie adaptation to economic realities and subsidize inefficiency and conspicuously to favor particular segments of the community at the camouflaged expense of the rest of the group. For the better part of two centuries, economists have understood the rationale of international specialization and trade, and well nigh unanimously they have adopted the logic as the basis of trade policy proposals. But blatant attempts are perennially made, by many representatives of both business and labor, to impose restrictions on foreign commerce—generally in the name of "fair" competition and "reasonable" wages.

Efforts to circumscribe the market and guide market activity are not confined to tariffs, quotas, and constricting "gentlemen's agreements." Government is as adept in messing up the realm of international finance as that of international trade.

Over the past half century and more, the world has compiled a lamentable history of exchange controls, pegging of exchange rates, and regulations on international investment. Following the international commercial and financial warfare of the 1930s, the rejection of the self-equilibrating foreign exchange market was institutionalized in the International Monetary Fund after World War II, until acceptance of a semi-free market was forced by a thoroughly deteriorated situation a decade ago.

Foreign exchange markets are genuine markets, and exchange rates are genuine prices. Market-determined prices clear markets; government-imposed prices yield shortages and surpluses, whether the market is for potatoes in the domestic economy or for dollars in the international economy. With market-determined exchange rates, there are no balance of payments crises. This elemental message has been propounded by Milton Friedman for a third of a century. It is now— belatedly—widely understood by analysts.

A. Trade, Protectionism, and Embargoes

In Defense of Dumping

February 20, 1978

At the recent annual convention of the AFL-CIO, president George Meany made an impassioned plea for government intervention to "protect American industry from cutthroat and often illegal foreign competition." Tariffs, quotas, agreements to restrict imports—anything to preserve the jobs of his members. The plea has great emotional appeal. What? Let those foreigners, willing to work for a pittance, take jobs from American workers? Let foreign firms subsidized by their governments "dump" products in the United States at the expense of American firms?

Before you swallow Mr. Meany's plea hook, line, and sinker, just ask yourself: who spoke at the AFL-CIO convention on behalf of the consumer, whom Meany would deprive of low-priced foreign goods? Who spoke on behalf of farmers or of workers in U.S. industries exporting goods overseas? After all, what's sauce for the goose is sauce for the gander. If we restrict imports, where are foreigners going to get dollars to pay for U.S. goods? If we restrict imports from them, can we complain if they restrict imports from us?

The Visible vs. the Invisible

Foreign trade is the classical example of an area in which public opinion tends to be biased by overemphasis on the visible as opposed to the invisible effects of government policy. The steelworkers whose jobs are threatened by steel imports from Japan are highly visible. They and their employers can see clearly the benefit to them from restricting imports of Japanese steel. The cost is large but spread thinly. Tens of thousands of buyers of objects made with steel would pay a bit more because of the restriction. The Japanese would earn fewer dollars here and, as a result, purchase fewer U.S. goods. But that cost too is invisible. The man who might have had a job producing a product the Japanese would have purchased if they had been permitted to sell more steel here will have no way of knowing that he has been hurt.

Workers who produce products that are sold to Japan to earn the yen used to buy Japanese steel are producing steel for the U.S. just as much as the men who tend to open-hearth furnaces in Gary. We could produce bananas in hot-houses, and no doubt would do so commercially if the tariff on bananas was high enough. Would that make sense? Obviously not—we can produce them more efficiently indirectly by trading export goods for bananas from Central America. It makes no more sense to provide a financial hothouse for the steel industry.

The U.S. gains from imports, not exports. Imports contribute to our standard of living. Exports are a cost. They are what we have to pay for the imports. The larger the volume of imports we can get for each unit of exports the better.

In the same way, we work to live, we do not live to work. Employment is a means to an end. It is a means to the production of goods and services that we can enjoy. Full employment is an empty objective if it means employment at unproductive jobs, digging holes for others to fill. The true

362

goal is widely shared *productive* employment, and again, the more output we can get from a given amount of work, the better.

The One and the Many

The upside-down view that makes exporting appear to be the goal of foreign trade and employment the goal of domestic policy arises because each of us tends to be involved in producing a single good or service, whereas we consume many thousands. Our interests as producers are concentrated, as consumers, diffused.

This bias is universal. The Japanese hurt themselves, and us, when they interfere with free trade by restricting imports or by subsidizing exports. But we can only increase the hurt to us, and to them, if we retaliate by following an equally unwise policy.

As Adam Smith wrote over 200 years ago in his great treatise, *The Wealth of Nations*: "What is prudence in the conduct of every private family, can scarce be folly in that of a great Kingdom. If a foreign country can supply us with a commodity cheaper than we ourselves can make it, better buy it of them with some part of the produce of our own industry, employed in a way in which we have some advantage. The general industry of the country . . . will not thereby be diminished . . . but only left to find out the way in which it can be employed to the greatest advantage."

Autos and Import Curbs

March 16, 1981

The Secretary of Transportation has been reported as making comments on automobile imports that are in sharp contrast with the philosophy expressed persistently and eloquently by the president whom he serves. Ronald Reagan has long been dedicated to expanding the role of the free market and reducing the role of government. He favors leaving individuals free to control their own lives, whether as consumers, workers, employers, or investors, provided that they do not interfere with the right of others to a similar freedom.

Secretary Drew Lewis has been reported as saying that the pace of automobile imports is unacceptable and that the administration is considering curbing them. He indicated that import curbs would be recommended only if "everybody brings something to the table." Unions, he said, would have to commit themselves to wage cuts and auto concerns to major capital investment devoted to manufacturing cars and parts in the United States.

Who Decides? Who would make sure that "everybody brings something to the table," decide whether that "something" was

364

enough, and enforce the subsequent collusive agreement? Clearly, the U.S. government, offering the carrot of restricting imports and wielding the whip of imposing regulatory controls: in other words, central-government planning of the automobile industry, administered by a government-union-industry consortium. The result would be a major reduction in the freedom of individuals as consumers, workers, employers, and investors.

The automobile industry is in deep trouble—in large part from actions of the U.S. government. By keeping the price of gasoline artificially low until recently, the government prolonged a market situation that was unfavorable to the domestic production of small cars. Attempts by automobile manufacturers to produce small, gas-efficient cars go back to the attempts by American Motors decades ago. But small cars never succeeded in the market so long as gasoline was relatively cheap. In addition, the government has imposed a host of costly regulations and controls on the industry. However, the way to remedy past regulatory mistakes is not to add new controls—that is the reaction of the alcoholic who turns to "more of the hair of the dog that bit him" to ease his hangover.

The issue is philosophical. But it is also eminently practical. The measures reportedly discussed by Secretary Lewis would do great harm. Consumers would be denied the freedom to buy whatever automobiles they regard as the best value for the money, wherever produced. Workers in export industries would lose jobs because, by reducing the number of dollars earned by foreigners, restrictions on imports would also reduce the number of dollars foreigners spend in the United States. The consumers and workers harmed earn on the average not much more than half as much as workers in the automobile industry—the only workers who might gain. So the measures reportedly discussed by Secretary Lewis would require low-paid workers to subsidize high-paid workers.

The economy as a whole would be harmed by forcing investment into channels determined by politics rather than productivity, and even more by reducing competition and reinforcing the unfortunate practice on the part of government of bailing out any large enterprises that make losses. Apparently, only small and politically weak enterprises must meet the market test.

Losses, No; Profits, Yes? But, it will be said, what about the mammoth losses of the automobile companies? If they justify intervention, what about the mammoth profits in years gone by and, we trust, in years to come? If losses are to be socialized, can profits be far behind?

The economic miracle that has been the United States was not produced by socialized enterprises, by government-union-industry cartels or by centralized economic planning. It was produced by private enterprises in a profit-and-loss system. And losses were at least as important in weeding out failures as profits in fostering successes. Let government succor failures, and we shall be headed for stagnation and decline.

If Secretary Lewis was reported accurately, I hope he spoke in a fit of absentmindedness. Let government help the automobile industry by correcting its past mistakes and by reducing the regulatory burden that it imposes. Beyond that, let the free market reign. And may the best autos win.

'Voluntary' Restrictions

April 6, 1981

The surge of Japanese auto imports into the United States has led to a growing pressure from top industry executives, government officials, and legislators for "voluntary" restraints on the part of Japan. Even Roger Smith, the new chairman of General Motors Corporation, the one automobile company that had consistently backed free trade in autos, has joined the clamor for voluntary restrictions.

Hypocrisy: Needless to say, the talk of voluntary restrictions is hypocrisy pure and simple. Japanese exporters are not about to cut their own throats "voluntarily." They will restrict exports only if their government requires them to do so—whether openly and explicitly or by more subtle means of persuasion. And the Japanese government will require them to restrict exports only if our government pressures or bribes Japan to do so.

The feature of voluntary restrictions that appeals to the automobile industry is at the same time one of the strongest arguments against the measure: such restrictions can be negotiated by executive action; and opposition to them can be more easily muzzled and circumvented than opposition to legislated restrictions. In short, voluntary restrictions are a form of taxation without representation.

I use the word "taxation" advisedly. Consider a tariff on Japanese cars—a straight tax. The higher the tax, the more expensive Japanese cars would be, and the fewer the number of cars that would be imported. Suppose the tax were high enough to limit Japanese imports to say, 1.6 million cars, roughly the number being talked about as the voluntary limit. Such a tax would yield revenue to the government from the imported cars. But it would make domestically produced as well as imported cars more expensive. Faced with less competition, domestic producers would be able to charge higher prices. So the cost to consumers would be greater, and in this case much greater, than the revenue to the government. The difference would be an imposed transfer from purchasers of cars to producers of cars.

Consider now a voluntary restriction of Japanese car exports to precisely the same number of cars. The effect on car prices in the United States would be identical. The maximum price at which 1.6 million Japanese cars can be sold is the same whether those cars have been subject to a tariff or not, and there is no reason why car dealers of Japanese firms should sell them for a lower price. Similarly, the lessened competition for domestic cars depends only on the reduction in the number of cars imported, not on how that reduction is brought about. However, if the reduction is brought about by voluntary restriction instead of a tariff, the U.S. government would get no revenue. Instead, that same revenue would be garnered by the Japanese—perhaps by the Japanese government if it cut exports by imposing an export tax, perhaps to the exporters fortunate enough to get export permits, perhaps by the officials in charge of doling out the export permits.

Scandal: This is by no means a purely hypothetical scenario. For years, for example, the United States and Taiwan have negotiated quotas on garments shipped from Taiwan to the United States: knit shirts, woven shirts, sweaters, pants, and dresses, with each type further classified by fiber content (cotton, wool, synthetic fiber). The quotas have become negotiable items and are bought and sold. The U.S. consumer pays a higher price, just as if a tariff had been levied, but the U.S. government gets no revenue from the phantom tariff, and the consumer is not aware that a tariff has been levied. Instead, the Taiwanese fortunate enough to be assigned quotas receive a windfall gain at the expense of American consumers and of other Taiwanese workers and manufacturers. A scandal, and yet it goes on year after year.

I oppose restrictions of any kind, legislated or voluntary. But if there are to be restrictions, let us be honest and open about them, not seek to achieve by subterfuge what an administration dedicated to promoting free trade and reliance on the market would find it embarrassing to support through legislation.

Economic Sanctions

January 21, 1980

A central feature of economic markets is the subtlety with which they connect producers and consumers and the anonymity in which they clothe the participants. That feature frustrates private individuals who wish to discriminate through the market. The racist who wishes to discriminate against blacks or whites, the anti-Semite who wishes to discriminate against Jews, the Christian who wishes to discriminate against Muslims, the Muslim who wishes to discriminate against Christians—all alike are foiled. The purchaser of bread cannot know whether the wheat from which it is baked was grown by a black or a white, a Jew, a Christian, or a Muslim.

Market Anonymity . . . The anonymity is less complete when nations are participants in the market, but it is still very real. That is why economic sanctions have seldom been effective. Even OPEC—which has so far proved an exception to the long-tested fragility of international cartels—is no exception to this proposition. The oil-price hikes of 1973 stuck but the attempt to embargo shipments to the U.S. failed. Oil is fungible and so are most other major articles of international commerce.

Rhodesia—a small, landlocked country—flourished for years despite the economic sanctions imposed on it. It managed to sell its products, to import needed materials, and to increase its output and productivity. Armed guerrilla warfare—not economic sanctions—destroyed its stability.

What of the proposed sanctions on Russia? Consider the limitation on exports of grain. President Carter has announced that the government will buy up the 17 million tons of grain that are to be diverted from Russia and remove them from the world market. Suppose, in addition, the U.S. government succeeded in persuading all other countries to join in the embargo and that they, in turn, enforced the embargo on their residents effectively.

In that most favorable case for President Carter's action, the embargo would deprive Russia of the grain without altering the world price of grain or the allocation of grain among the countries other than Russia. Russia would lose the grain; the American taxpayers would pay the corresponding sum for grain they would not otherwise have bought—or, to put it differently, they would get the grain instead of the goods that could have been acquired with the proceeds of the aborted sale.

But this case will not occur. Many countries, in the Soviet bloc and outside it, will not join the embargo. And those countries that do join the embargo will not be able to enforce it effectively—any more than Britain and the U.S. were able to enforce sanctions against Rhodesia.

In that case, federal purchases of grain will simply be a net addition to the world's demand for grain, while Russia buys its grain elsewhere. The initial decline in grain prices in response to the embargo will be converted into a modest rise in the world prices of grain because of the additional demand. U.S. farmers would be benefited, not hurt, because the price in the U.S. would rise along with the world price, as would exports to countries other than Russia. U.S. consumers would be hurt doubly—once as taxpayers, once as purchasers of wheat. Consumers in other countries would also be hurt. As to Russia, it would be hurt too because it would have to pay a few percent more for wheat plus the extra cost of rerouting grain shipments. In short, the net effect would be a gain to the world's producers of grain, financed partly by Russia but mostly by non-Russian purchasers of grain and U.S. taxpayers.

High-technology products are less fungible than wheat, so in principle it should be easier to enforce an embargo on them. However, the difference is likely to be minor. Items shipped to one country can readily be reshipped elsewhere. In addition, we are not the only country producing such products. On the contrary, we have been losing ground in this area in the world marketplace. Insofar as there is any effect of an embargo on sales by U.S. enterprises, it will probably be to hasten their decline as producers of such products.

. . . Protects Russia: All in all, economic sanctions are not an effective weapon of political warfare. They are likely to do us as much harm as they do their intended target, not only in the ways already mentioned but also by weakening the system of free markets that is our greatest source of strength.

The resort to economic sanctions is a confession of impotence, crafted primarily for domestic consumption, to reassure the public. It will have little or no influence on the Russians.

B. The Balance of Payments and the Value of Currencies

Exchange-Rate Jitters

September 5, 1977

The recent hysteria about the balance of payments reflects primarily a cultural lag.

A similar flurry in the exchange markets in 1970, say, would have been extremely serious. At that time, most leading countries were seeking to maintain fixed exchange rates—that is to say, fixed prices for each currency in terms of the others. A balance-of-payments "deficit" would have led not to a change in the price of the dollar in terms of the mark or the franc but to purchases of dollars at the official price by the German Bundesbank, the Bank of France, and other central banks. They would have been willing to buy dollars because the U.S. government was committed to selling them gold at a fixed dollar price. Hence, they could replace unwanted dollars by gold at their pleasure. Faced with the possibility of a large call for gold, the U.S. would have had to take drastic measures to stem the run.

Such a run on the dollar in August 1971 finally led President Nixon to close the gold window and set the dollar free—measures that were long overdue.

Changed Circumstances

Today, there are no "official" exchange rates for the dollar—except as other countries may choose to peg their currencies to the dollar. If the German Bundesbank now buys dollars, it is speculating strictly on its own; it has no commitment from the U.S. or anyone else to bail it out.

Under these circumstances, there literally is no such thing as a "balance-of-payments problem." Suppose, as now, U.S. residents want to spend more dollars on foreign goods and services than foreign residents want to spend on U.S. goods and services. To do so, U.S. residents must acquire extra foreign currency. They can do so from income on foreign investments, by borrowing abroad, or by selling securities abroad, or by using up balances of foreign currency. If these sources are not adequate at some initial exchange rate, then U.S. seekers for foreign currencies will bid up their price, in the process reducing the amount of foreign currencies they or others seek to acquire and increasing the amount available—just as the price of wheat is bid up if the quantity demanded is greater than the amount available. There is no need for intervention by government.

But, you may ask, doesn't the "deficit" mean that we are dissipating our substance, borrowing from the future to consume today—notably OPEC oil? It may, but it need not. Some items U.S. residents buy abroad are for investment, not consumption—for example, goods and services imported to build factories or houses here. An excess of purchases over sales abroad is entirely consistent with an accumulation of capital assets at home and abroad.

Unchanged Attitudes

The cultural lag shows up in the exaggerated attention paid by the news media to trivial changes in exchange rates. A recent headline in the *Wall Street Journal* read: POUND

EASES. It turned out that the price of the pound had gone from $1.7381 to $1.7380. Had it gone to $1.7371, no doubt the *Journal* headline would have read: POUND PLUMMETS.

In a world of floating rates, the price of the dollar in terms of other currencies is a market price fluctuating from day to day, going up with respect to some currencies, down with respect to others. At the height of the recent fuss about the weakness of the dollar, the average value of the U.S. dollar* was 3.7 percent higher than on December 14, 1973, and less than one-half of 1 percent lower than at the end of 1976. As I write, the average value has more than recovered this loss.

These averages are not a reason for self-congratulation. On the contrary, all they show is that over the past four years our inflation has been a trifle less than the average of our trading partners and is currently about the same. We do have a real dollar problem. But that problem is the internal value of the dollar, not its external value. Inflation has been eroding the purchasing power of the dollar. Inflation continues, and threatens to accelerate. If we tended to our domestic affairs and followed policies that would maintain the internal value of the dollar, we could forget about its external value. The market would take care of that.

---

*Computed by Morgan Guaranty Trust Co. as a weighted average of different exchange rates, using as a weight for each exchange rate U.S. trade with the country in question.

The Pound Crisis

October 11, 1976

There is no mystery why the British pound has been plummeting in price. The mystery is why the British government has been wasting its taxpayers' money in futile speculation against the decline.

How much a British pound is worth in dollars depends fundamentally on how much a pound will buy in goods and services and how much a dollar will buy. If a pound will buy as much as $2 will buy, the pound is worth $2. If a pound will buy only as much as $1 will buy, the pound is worth $1. Of course, this principle is easier to state than to apply. Some goods and services may cost three times as much in the U.S. in dollars as they cost in Britain in pounds; others may cost less in dollars than in pounds. The mythical average is not readily observed—except in the dollar value that the market sets on the pound.

Given the dollar value of the pound at any time, if British prices in pounds rise faster than U.S. prices in dollars, the dollar value of the pound will go down. That is what has been happening. Prices have for years been rising more rapidly in Britain than in the U.S. For the two years from February 1974 to February 1976 prices rose 22 percent per year in Britain, less than 9 percent per year in the U.S.; in the next six months at the annual rate of 13 percent in Britain, 6 percent in the U.S. Is it any wonder that the dollar value of the British pound has been declining?

The real mystery is why the British government some time back borrowed $5 billion from an international consortium to support the pound; and why, now that a new crisis has arisen, it is seeking to borrow an additional sum from the International Monetary Fund even though $4 billion of the original loan remains unused. The history of such exchange-rate propping ventures is crystal-clear; none has ever succeeded except as part of a major internal economic and monetary reform which had real promise of ending inflation and in fact succeeded in doing so. For the rest, as in earlier British devaluations, the venture has stemmed the decline for a time but, after a brief interval, has had to be given up and the currency in question has then plummeted.

Attempts to prevent a currency from appreciating, such as those undertaken by Germany and Japan, have had the same fate. The attempt succeeds for a time but soon must be given up as futile, and each of these episodes of governmental exchange speculation has been costly to taxpayers.

Paying to Fool the Voter

In the present instance, the British government has spent about $1 billion of its earlier loan buying pounds at about $1.80 a pound supposedly to keep the pound from falling. To get the dollars to repay the loan, Britain will now have to sell pounds at about $1.60 to $1.65 a pound, at a cost to the taxpayers of the difference—or about $100 million of taxpayers' money squandered in futile speculation.

The British experts know the history of such ventures as well as I do. They could have had no illusions about the results of their actions—that, presumably, is why they spent only $1 billion of the first loan before turning to IMF.

Why then did they do it, knowing that they would only postpone the decline in the price of the pound and then very likely produce a crisis?

My conjecture—and I emphasize it is only a conjecture—is that they did it for the same reason that large industrial concerns hire outside consultants to advise them to take unpleasant measures that management knows very well need to be taken.

The British government knows that the only way to stem inflation is for government to spend less and to create less money. But these measures are unpleasant and the British government does not have the courage or integrity, or, to be more generous, the political support to take them on its own. It has therefore spent $100 million of its taxpayers' money to give it an excuse to call in the IMF money doctors—since it is standard practice for the IMF to attach conditions about internal fiscal and monetary policies.

The British government will huff and puff about the conditions. But it will also welcome the exchange crisis and the IMF's insistence on conditions as a way to put the blame for unpleasant measures on outside consultants rather than on its own past mismanagement.

Borrowing Marks

January 8, 1979

What is likely to happen to the value of the dollar in terms of the German mark? According to the U.S. Treasury, the recent decline in value will continue, but the decline will be moderate, not more than about 3 percent a year, on the average of the next three or four years. German investors agree that the decline will continue, but they expect it to average much more than 3 percent a year.

Actions vs. Words

How do I know what the U.S. Treasury expects? Not from what the Secretary of the Treasury says. Secretary Michael Blumenthal testified recently before the Congressional Joint Economic Committee that "we will see a further strengthening" in the American currency. But actions speak louder than words. At the same time that Secretary Blumenthal was testifying to Congress, the Treasury borrowed $1.6 billion in Germany in the form of securities denominated in marks. It offered to pay an interest rate of roughly 6 percent per year on mark-denominated three- and four-year securities. On comparable securities denominated in dollars, the Treasury is currently paying a bit over 9 percent—or 3 percentage points per year more.

These two forms of borrowing will be equal in cost if, and only if, the price of the dollar in terms of the mark falls by 3 percent a year. The lower interest rate in marks would then be just offset by the greater number of dollars required to redeem the securities. If the dollar depreciates less than 3 percent a year or appreciates, borrowing in marks will cost less than borrowing in dollars. On the other hand, if the dollar depreciates more than 3 percent a year, the Treasury will have made a bad deal.

The situation is of course reversed for lenders: they gain by lending in marks rather than dollars if the dollar depreciates by more than 3 percent a year. They expressed in no uncertain terms their belief that the dollar would depreciate more by offering to lend nearly three times as many marks as the Treasury was willing to borrow.

The Treasury did not borrow in marks to save interest. It did so as part of a package of dollar-strengthening measures announced by President Carter on November 1. The Treasury's own lack of confidence that those measures plus future government actions will succeed in preventing depreciation in the dollar is demonstrated not only by the interest rates that the Treasury offered but also by its unwillingness to borrow as many marks as Germans were willing to lend. In addition, the Treasury restricted the security issue to German lenders—demonstrating its unwillingness to offer Americans the same opportunity to speculate against the dollar that it has offered Germans and plans to offer the Swiss.

Does borrowing in foreign currencies strengthen the dollar? Initially, yes. The borrowed currencies are used to buy dollars, which does tend to raise the price of the dollar. But that effect is necessarily transitory. When the debt is repaid, dollars will have to be sold to buy marks, which will tend to lower the price of the dollar. At best, such borrowing can only buy time for more fundamental actions. And it may not do even that, since there are many offsets. For example, some investors may have acquired marks to lend by selling dollar securities or might have bought dollar securities had the mark-dominated securities not been available. All in all, I believe that such borrowing will have a negligible effect on the price of the dollar and will ultimately cost the American taxpayer heavily.

The Real Problem

Borrowing in marks is both unwise and unnecessary. It is unwise because it involves the U.S. government in speculation, the outcome of which depends on many events outside its control, such as German economic policy. It is unnecessary because if the U.S. government took credible measures to deal with the fundamental sources of dollar weaknesses, the speculators of the world would provide the funds to bolster the dollar until those measures took hold.

The dollar is weak abroad because it is weak at home. It is weak at home because the U.S. government has been spending too much, and creating too much money to finance its spending. The way to strengthen the dollar abroad is to strengthen it at home. And fundamentally there is only one way to do that: not by talk, not by promises, not by cosmetic borrowing abroad, but by less government spending and less creation of money.

C. Two International Case Studies

Japan and Inflation

September 4, 1978

To judge from the Washington babel, inflation can arise from many sources; the classical medicine for fighting inflation no longer works; we must advise new and more sophisticated cures.

This talk is mostly a smoke screen generated by our natural propensity to blame someone else for our own failings. The truth is:

1. Substantial inflation is a monetary phenomenon, almost always arising from a more rapid increase in the quantity of money than in output (though, of course, the reasons for the increase in money may be various).

2. In today's world, government determines—or can determine—the quantity of money.

3. There is only one fundamental cure for inflation: a slower rate of increase in the quantity of money.

4. It takes time—measured in years, not months—for inflation to develop; it takes time for inflation to be cured.

Change in Policy

Japan's recent experience provides an almost textbook illustration of these simple truths. As the chart shows, the quantity of money in Japan began growing at higher and higher rates in 1971. By mid-1973, it was growing more than 25 percent a year. The reason: a policy of trying to maintain a fixed exchange rate for the yen in terms of the dollar. There was upward pressure on the yen then as now. To counter this pressure, the Japanese authorities bought dollars with newly created yen, which added to the money supply. In principle, they could have offset this addition to the money supply by other measures, but they did not do so.

Inflation did not respond until about two years later, in early 1973. The subsequent dramatic rise in inflation, plus

**INFLATION FOLLOWS MONEY:
THE CASE OF JAPAN**

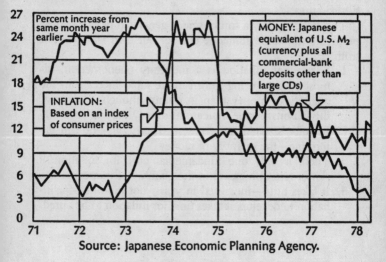

Percent increase from same month year earlier

MONEY: Japanese equivalent of U.S. M₂ (currency plus all commercial-bank deposits other than large CDs)

INFLATION: Based on an index of consumer prices

Source: Japanese Economic Planning Agency.

the influence of the present Prime Minister, Takeo Fukuda, then Minister of Finance, produced a fundamental change in monetary policy. Emphasis was shifted from the external value of the yen—the exchange rate—to its internal value— inflation. Monetary growth was reduced sharply, from more than 25 percent a year to between 10 and 15 percent. It has been kept there, with minor exceptions, ever since. (In Japan's special circumstances, monetary growth at the top of this range would produce roughly stable prices. The comparable rate for the U.S. is 3 to 5 percent.)

About eighteen months after monetary growth started down, inflation followed suit, but it took two and a half years before inflation fell below double digits. Inflation then held roughly constant for about two years—despite a mild upturn in monetary growth. More recently, inflation has started moving rapidly toward zero in response to a new decline in monetary growth.

The numbers on inflation in the chart are only for consumer prices. Wholesale prices have been doing even better. They have actually been declining for more than a year. The postwar shift of workers in Japan from low-productivity to high-productivity sectors has meant that prices of services have risen sharply relative to prices of commodities. As a result, consumer prices have risen relative to wholesale prices.

How Long? At What Cost?

Japan's experience throws light on two persistent questions: How long would it take to control inflation in the U.S.? What would be the interim effects on output and employment? How long? Two to five years.

Interim Effects on Output and Employment? The initial spurt of Japanese monetary growth in 1972 and early 1973 temporarily produced high rates of growth of output, but then, as monetary growth declined but inflation gathered speed, Japan went into a slump, reaching the low point at the end of 1974. When inflation finally started to fall, output began recovering and has been growing ever since—at a more modest rate than in the boom years of the 1960s but at a highly respectable one nonetheless: more than 5 percent per year.

Four times in the past twenty years, the U.S. has gone through the first phase—rising, then falling, monetary growth; increasing inflation, and recession. Each time, as in Japan, that phase has been followed by declining inflation and a modest recovery. But, unfortunately, we have not had the patience to continue monetary restraint. Instead, we have overreacted. We have stepped again on the monetary accelerator and have set off on another round of inflation, condemning ourselves to higher inflation plus higher unemployment.

Japan's persistence in a policy of noninflationary monetary growth does its leaders and the people of Japan great credit. The contrast with U.S. economic policy offers a far better explanation of why the Japanese yen continues to appreciate relative to the dollar than do alleged subsidies by the Japanese government to exporters, Japan Incorporated, "wicked" speculators, and the host of other largely irrelevant factors that are all the talk of Washington.

Free Markets and the Generals

January 25, 1982

The adoption of free-market policies by Chile with the blessing and support of the military junta headed by General Pinochet has given rise to the myth that only an authoritarian regime can successfully implement a free-market policy.

The facts are very different. Chile is an exception, not the rule. The military is hierarchical and its personnel are imbued with the tradition that some give and some obey orders: it is organized from the top down. A free market is the reverse. It is voluntaristic, authority is dispersed; bargaining, not submission to orders, is its watchword; it is organized from the bottom up.

Military juntas in other South American countries have been as authoritarian in the economic sphere as they have been in politics. So were General Franco and the Greek colonels. Some have introduced free-market elements to meet an economic crisis—but so did Russia in the 1920s with its new economic policy and so has China in recent years. However, to the best of my knowledge, none, with the exception of Chile, has supported a fully free-market economy as a matter of principle.

Miracles: Chile is an economic miracle. Inflation has been cut from 700 percent a year in mid-1974 to less than 10 percent a year. After a difficult transition, the economy boomed, growing an average of about 8 percent a year from 1976 to 1980. Real wages and employment rose rapidly and unemployment fell. Imports and exports surged after export subsidies were eliminated and tariffs were slashed to a flat 10 percent (except for temporarily higher rates for most automobiles). Many state enterprises have been denationalized and motor transport and other areas deregulated. A voucher system has been put into effect in elementary and secondary education. Most remarkable of all, a social-security reform has been adopted that permits individuals to choose between participating in the government system or providing for their own retirement privately.

Chile is an even more amazing political miracle. A military regime has supported reforms that reduce sharply the role of the state and replace control from the top with control from the bottom.

This political miracle is the product of an unusual set of circumstances. The chaos produced by the Allende regime that precipitated the military takeover in 1973 discredited central economic control. In an attempt to rectify the situation, the military drew on a comprehensive plan for a free-market economy that had been prepared by a group of young Chilean economists, most, though not all, of whom had studied at the University of Chicago. For the first two years, the so-called "Chicago boys" participated in implementing the plan but only in subordinate positions, and there was little progress in reducing inflation. Somewhat in desperation, the junta turned major responsibility over to the Chicago boys. Fortunately, several of them combined outstanding intellectual and executive ability with the courage of their convictions and a sense of dedication to implementing them—and the economic miracle was on its way.

Chile is currently having serious difficulties—along with much of the rest of the world. And the opposition to the free-market policies that had been largely silenced by success is being given full voice—from both inside and outside the military. This temporary setback will likely be surmounted. But I predict that the free-market policy will not last unless the military government is replaced by a civilian government dedicated to political liberty—as the junta has announced is its intention. Otherwise, sooner or later—and probably sooner rather than later—economic freedom will succumb to the authoritarian character of the military.

Liberty: A civilian government, too, might destroy the free market—after all, Allende was doing so in Chile when he was overthrown by the military. Yet it is no accident that the spread of the free market in the nineteenth century was accompanied by the widening of political liberty and that, although politically free societies have moved in the direction of collectivism, none has gone all the way except through the force of arms.

I have long argued that economic freedom is a necessary but not sufficient condition for political freedom. I have become persuaded that this generalization, while true, is misleading unless accompanied by the proposition that political freedom in turn is a necessary condition for the long-term maintenance of economic freedom.